Exploration Into AUSTRALIA

KATE DARIAN-SMITH

 *Belitha Press*

Belitha Press in association with the Royal Geographic Society

Foreword

Previous page: **T**he sugar gum trees and red cliffs of Mount Remarkable National Park, Flinders Ranges, South Australia.

This page: **A**n artist's impression of Uluru (Ayers Rock). To see what Uluru really looks like turn to page 6.

Many animals, birds and fish regularly travel over great distances. What sets people apart is the ability to explore and discover. An explorer is someone who is curious about the world and if you are curious enough to read this book then you too have become an explorer.

Exploring is not just about getting into a plane or sailing on a boat to a place you have never been before – you have to record what you see, listen to the people you meet and learn about the place you find. This book follows in the footsteps of all good explorers by discovering the people, history and countryside of the land before it was 'discovered' by outside peoples as well as telling the stories of the adventurers who travelled there for the first time.

Explorers have travelled all over the world and have been helped throughout the centuries by the inhabitants of the lands they visited. People have shown outsiders their homes, helped them carry their loads, paddled their canoes, showed them amazing animals and often housed, clothed, fed, rescued and cured them. This book tells you about these people as well as the explorers they helped or fought with.

Travellers have explored the world for many different reasons. Early adventurers like Marco Polo (1254-1324) and Ibn Battuta (1304-1364) journeyed with trading caravans. Christopher Columbus (1451-1506), Ferdinand Magellan (1480-1521), Captain James Cook (1728-1779) and John Franklin (1786-1847) were sent by governments to investigate the geography of the world. Other explorers were merchants, scientists, colonialists, artists, adventurers, naturalists or even conquerors like Francisco Pizarro (1475-1541) who destroyed the Inca Empire that he discovered.

The Royal Geographical Society is proud to support the *Exploration Into* series of books. Ever since it was founded in 1830, the RGS has helped and inspired famous explorers like Robert Scott (1868-1912) and Dr David Livingstone (1813-1873). Today, the RGS helps modern-day explorers climb the world's mountains, walk across its deserts, cycle through its continents, sail up its rivers, dive deep under the oceans and discover the scientific secrets of nature. We invite you to pick up *Exploration Into* and start your own journey of discovery . . .

DR JOHN HEMMING, *Director and Secretary, Royal Geographical Society, London*

Contents

Aboriginal dancers paint their bodies as a part of their performances.

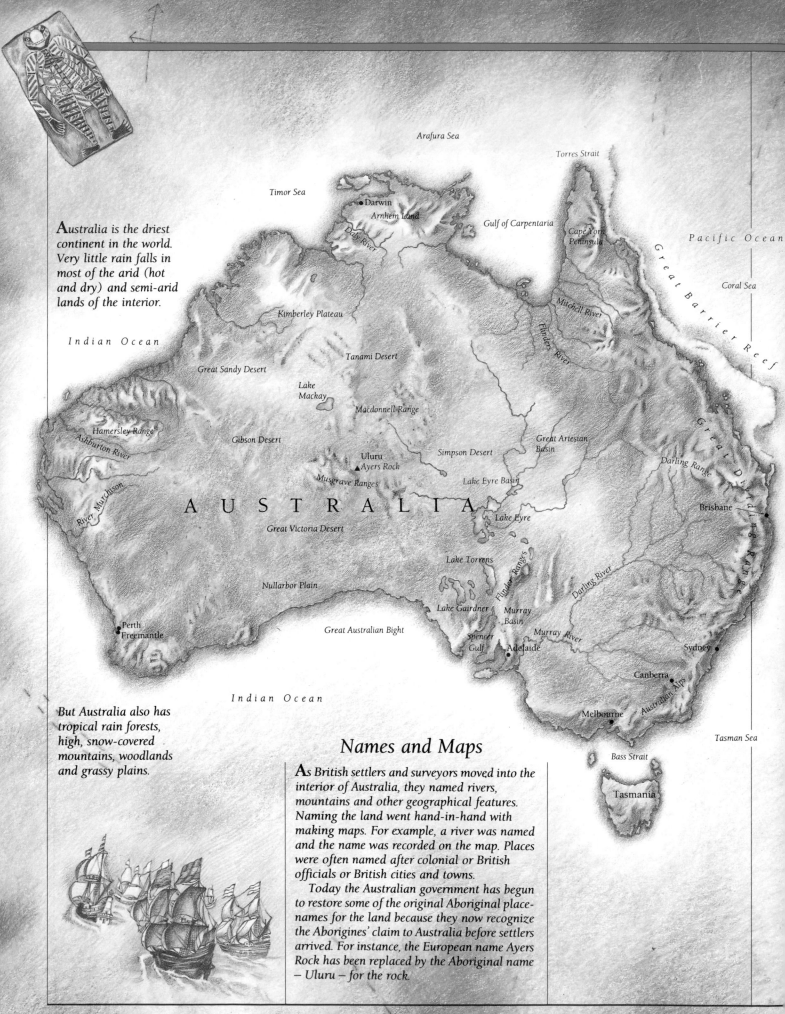

Australia is the driest continent in the world. Very little rain falls in most of the arid (hot and dry) and semi-arid lands of the interior.

But Australia also has tropical rain forests, high, snow-covered mountains, woodlands and grassy plains.

Arafura Sea

Torres Strait

Timor Sea

Darwin

Arnhem Land

Daly River

Gulf of Carpentaria

Cape York Peninsula

Pacific Ocean

Coral Sea

Kimberley Plateau

Mitchell River

Flinders River

Indian Ocean

Great Sandy Desert

Tanami Desert

Lake Mackay

Macdonnell Range

Hamersley Range

Ashburton River

Gibson Desert

Great Artesian Basin

Great Barrier Reef

Darling Range

Uluru
Ayers Rock

Simpson Desert

River Murchison

Musgrave Ranges

Lake Eyre Basin

AUSTRALIA

Great Dividing Range

Brisbane

Great Victoria Desert

Lake Eyre

Lake Torrens

Flinders Ranges

Darling River

Nullarbor Plain

Lake Gairdner

Murray Basin

Perth
Freemantle

Great Australian Bight

Spencer Gulf

Adelaide

Murray River

Sydney

Canberra

Australian Alps

Indian Ocean

Melbourne

Tasman Sea

Bass Strait

Tasmania

Names and Maps

As British settlers and surveyors moved into the interior of Australia, they named rivers, mountains and other geographical features. Naming the land went hand-in-hand with making maps. For example, a river was named and the name was recorded on the map. Places were often named after colonial or British officials or British cities and towns.

Today the Australian government has begun to restore some of the original Aboriginal place-names for the land because they now recognize the Aborigines' claim to Australia before settlers arrived. For instance, the European name Ayers Rock has been replaced by the Aboriginal name – Uluru – for the rock.

1 Exploring Australia

The Story of Australia

For centuries before they actually 'discovered' and settled the mysterious continent of Australia, European people imagined that great riches were to be found there. But Aborigines had been living in Australia for more than 50,000 years by the time Europeans trekked across the continent in search of gold and land for grazing animals and growing crops.

Different Histories

Different peoples have different ways of remembering and recording the past. There is no single history of a country or its peoples – what you believe depends upon your point of view and your present circumstances. Many Australians think of the heroism of white explorers and settlers as being their history. But the Aboriginal groups who lost their land when white people came to explore and settle Australia think of these explorers as invaders rather than brave heroes.

Until recently, almost all Australian history was about the experiences of white **immigrants**. Today, new history books are being written that include the experiences of Aboriginal peoples and non-European people who travelled to Australia to live and work. This book looks at some of the different histories of the exploration of Australia.

Exploring this Book

This book is divided into seven chapters. Chapters one and two explore the lives of Aboriginal peoples before white people settled in Australia in 1788. Chapters three and four follow the journeys of European and Asian visitors to Australia up to the late 1700s. Chapter five follows the journeys of the people who explored Australia's interior (middle). The conflict between white settlers and Aborigines is the subject of chapter six, and the book ends by looking at Australia's recent explorers.

Creation and Discovery

You would need to walk for nine kilometres to travel around the massive rock known as Uluru.

Archaeological evidence tells us that the ancestors of modern Aborigines arrived in Australia at least 50,000 years ago. Archaeologists have examined Aboriginal bones, stone tools, campsites and homes and have even found the fossilized remains of food that ancient Aborigines ate. But, unlike the scientists, traditional Aborigines believe that they have lived in Australia since the beginning of time. Aborigines call the beginning of time and the events which shaped their world the Dreamtime.

This Aboriginal rock carving from Ewaninga near Alice Springs is a record of Aboriginal history. Aboriginal rock carvings can be found all over Australia.

This is an Aboriginal axe-head made from flint.

Creation

Aboriginal history has been passed on from generation to generation by word of mouth. This is called oral history. Ancient Aboriginal societies did not write down stories, but remembered them in songs and in paintings on bark, rock or human bodies. In Aboriginal Australia, every group had its own long and complicated creation history related to its land. Aboriginal history is closely tied to religious beliefs about the creation of the land during the Dreamtime.

The Histories of the Dreamtime

Aborigines believe that during the Dreamtime **ancestral spirit beings** came from under the ground or out of the sky and travelled across the land creating mountains, valleys, rivers and deserts. They also made animals, birds, reptiles, fish, plants and people. The ancestral beings then gave Aboriginal people their laws and customs. Once they had finished their acts of creation, they disappeared into the sky or the sea or turned into parts of the land.

The Dreamtime is still the source of the songs, dances, art and **rituals** Aborigines use to express their religion. The Aborigines believe that they have to care for the places of **spiritual significance** left by their ancestral spirits. They also keep and adapt the laws and traditions that were first laid down by the spirit beings. Different Aboriginal creation stories are told by each group.

The Djanggau Sisters

The Aborigines of north-eastern Arnhem Land in the Northern Territory believe that human beings were created by the Djanggau Sisters.

The two Djanggau Sisters were ancestral spirit beings known as the Daughters of the Sun. Accompanied by their brother, they came in a bark canoe from a land far away over the sea called the Land of the Dead. Once at Arnhem Land, they created birds and trees, shaped the country and gave names to places. Most importantly, the sisters gave birth to the first humans.

The Crocodile Lake

The Aborigines of Narran Lake in New South Wales believe that the lake was made by two crocodile-like ancestral spirit beings. The crocodile-like beings were killed by the Ba'iame, a brave hunter, because they had eaten his wives. As they died, the crocodile creatures thrashed about and made a hollow in the ground that became the lake.

Naughty Spirit Beings

As well as the ancestral spirit beings, Aborigines believe that other spirits live on their lands. Some of these are naughty spirits, like the Net-nets in Victoria. The Net-nets hide things from people and trip people up but always manage to keep out of sight!

According to Aboriginal beliefs, there are other spirits that live on the land and are very powerful. For instance, the man-like spirit of Doologa is covered in hair and is found in the south coast regions of New South Wales. Children are warned that this spirit will capture them if they are naughty.

This traditional Aboriginal picture is painted with coloured ochre (see page 17) on a piece of bark. It shows the Waijara ancestral spirit being with a kangaroo and some fibre baskets (see page 13).

Aboriginal elders are responsible for teaching the histories of the Dreamtime to young people.

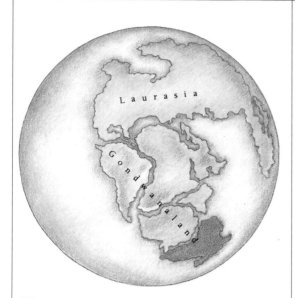

This is what the world looked like over 200 million years ago. The shaded area of land eventually became Australia.

We do not know what the first explorers to Australia looked like or what type of boats they used. This is an artist's impression of what these ancient travellers might have been like.

Gondwanaland

Over 200 million years ago all the land in the world formed one continent. Eventually the land started to break into two. Scientists think that 95 million years ago one half of these two supercontinents (called Gondwanaland) began to split into pieces. The continent of Australia was one of these pieces.

Voyages Across the Sea

Unlike traditional Aborigines, archaeologists and **prehistorians** do not believe that humans have always lived in Australia. So where did the first Australians come from? Archaeological evidence shows that people probably travelled from South East Asia to Australia at least 50,000 years ago. At that time, Australia and Asia were separated by sea. But the sea levels of the world were lower than they are now and more land was exposed. There was probably only about 100 kilometres between some of the islands of Indonesia and northern Australia. This was still a dangerous journey on a small raft or in a canoe. No one knows whether people came to Australia when their rafts and canoes were accidentally carried there by the ocean currents, or whether their voyages were planned.

Travelling Through the Land

When the first Australians arrived in northern Australia, they found a land with a hot, wet climate similar to that in South East Asia. Gradually, groups of people began to travel south to cooler areas. It took about 10,000 years for Aborigines to explore and settle the whole of Australia. Fifty thousand years ago, Australia was 20 per cent larger than it is now. It was joined to the islands of Papua New Guinea in the north and Tasmania in the south. The land became smaller as the sea level rose (because the **ice caps** melted, see page 10) and covered more of the coastline. Some scientists think that the sea has risen 150 metres in the last 50,000 years. But the land of ancient Australia was not that different from modern-day Australia. There were low mountains in the east, deserts in the centre, **marsupial** animals and eucalyptus or gum trees.

Tasmania separated from the Australian mainland 12,000 years ago. Papua New Guinea separated from Australia 8,000 years ago.

Radiocarbon Dating

Archaeologists use radiocarbon dating in their research into the ancient history of Australia. This is a technique which measures the level of radioactive carbon that is present in all natural things (such as shell, bone or wood). Because radioactive carbon breaks down and rots at a constant rate, it is possible to tell how old materials are by measuring how much they have decayed. Radiocarbon dating can be done on burnt materials like the shells found at Aboriginal campsites.

An archaeologist at work in Australia's outback. He is digging up fossils which will be radiocarbon dated in a laboratory.

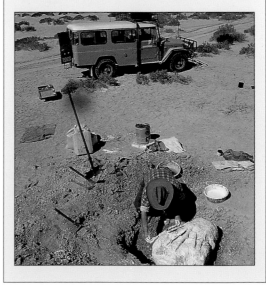

Occupying the Land

The ancestors of today's Aborigines had to be tough and intelligent to survive in Australia's wide range of temperatures, weather and environments. They also had to be able to use the land to suit their needs. During the last **Ice Age**, between 10,000 and 60,000 years ago, the world became much colder and drier. The Aborigines had to cope with massive temperature changes. Some land turned into desert and other areas became covered with rain forest.

Rising Seas

As the Earth's climate became warmer after the Ice Age, **glaciers** and the polar ice-caps began to melt. All this extra water made the level of the world's oceans rise. In some places the sea rose several metres in about ten years. Aborigines living on the coast of Australia were forced to explore inland as their land became covered in water. The oral histories of the coastal Aboriginal communities of northern Australia tell us about important Aboriginal ritual places which are now under the sea.

Australia has areas of swampland like the one above. Swamps provided plenty of food for Aboriginal groups, such as birds, fish and even crocodiles.

The Simpson Desert is a vast area of rolling sandhills. It is very difficult to find food in Australia's deserts, but Aborigines have managed to survive even here.

Wombats are stocky, round marsupials that grow to over one metre in length and can weigh as much as 40 kilograms.

Giant Kangaroos

The first Aborigines hunted animals that have now disappeared. These included diprotodonts, which were giant marsupials. There were also other giant marsupials such as wombats (above) and koalas. Many of these animals became **extinct** because the Aborigines hunted too many of them. Other animals became smaller over the centuries. Today's grey kangaroos can reach over two metres in height and today's wombats are relatives of the prehistoric wombats.

There are about fifty different types of kangaroo in Australia. This is a western grey kangaroo.

A photograph taken in 1878 of some Torres Strait islanders.

Torres Strait Islanders

Papua New Guinea became separated from the Australian mainland 8,000 years ago (at the same time as the islands of Great Britain and Ireland became separated from Europe) because of the rise in the sea's level. The tops of mountains and volcanoes that remained above the sea became islands in the Torres Strait. The Torres Strait between Australia and Papua New Guinea is about 145 kilometres wide. A new population grew up in Papua New Guinea and these people moved on to the surrounding islands. The islanders depended on the sea for their food, but grew some crops as well. The people who live on these islands are called Torres Strait Islanders and they are Australia's second group of **indigenous** people.

People from the eastern Torres Strait islands speak a Papuan language, while those from the western islands speak an Aboriginal language. Goods were exchanged across the Torres Strait between the Aborigines, Torres Strait Islanders and the Papuans.

The Great Barrier Reef is made up of reefs and islands. It runs along the east coast of Australia for 2,000 kilometres.

2 Australia Before 1788

Living with the Land

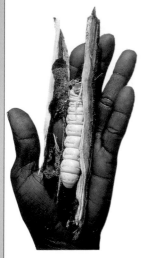

This is a witchetty grub. Aborigines eat these grubs both raw and cooked. Raw witchetty grubs taste like butter and cooked witchetty grubs taste like pork.

Aboriginal people have lived all over Australia. This chapter tells some of the stories of Aboriginal groups throughout Australia.

Living off the Land

The Aborigines moved through their lands as the climate and seasons changed. This way of life is called semi-nomadic. They usually travelled in families or clans. Everyone hunted or gathered food. Children were taught how to find food by the adults. The Aborigines knew which plants and animals could be eaten, how to find and catch them, and how to prepare them for eating. Medicines, clothing, shelters, weapons and tools were all made from plants and animals.

Sometimes the search for food only took two or three hours a day, but in dry countryside it could take much longer.

The Aborigines carefully farmed their plants. They scattered seeds and introduced new plants from similar landscapes elsewhere in Australia. They harvested some plants and replanted others to make sure that they would survive the harsh climate. They also prepared food so that it could be stored for the winter or when there was no rain to grow new plants.

This is a nineteenth-century photograph of a group of Aborigines in southern Australia. These people have probably painted themselves especially for the photographer. It is also likely that the photographer made the women wear European dresses.

An early European engraving of Aborigines hunting black swans.

Farming with Fire

Aborigines have been called 'fire-stick' farmers because they used fire to farm the land. Different parts of the country were set alight at certain times of the year or every few years. Burning the land protected certain trees from being strangled by weeds, encouraged new plants to grow, cleared out lizards and small animals, and preserved grasslands where grazing kangaroos and wallabies were hunted. Aborigines used their skill to control the spread and temperature of the fires. They also used fire to burn paths through dense forests to make travelling easier.

Tools and Weapons

The Aborigines used a wide variety of tools and weapons. Digging sticks were used to dig up **yams** and catch reptiles and small animals by cornering them in their burrows. They used clubs, spears and boomerangs to fight as well as to hunt. Boomerangs were used in games or to kill birds. The Aborigines fished from canoes and rafts in rivers or on the open sea.

Using Fibres

Hand-woven bags from Cape York.

Aborigines made many objects from the **fibres** of bark, leaves and plants. Plants were made into string or rope. String bags and woven or coiled baskets were used for storage. In the rain forests of north Queensland, large funnel-shaped traps made by twisting fibres together were used to catch small kangaroos called pademelons. In south-east Australia, eel traps were made from twined fibres. Aborigines hunted with nets throughout the eastern, southern and western parts of Australia.

Aboriginal men from Arnhem Land in northern Australia. They are dressed for an important ceremony.

How Many Aborigines?

In 1788, when the British invaded Australia, there were between 750,000 and three million Aboriginal people living there. They were members of about 650 different groups speaking about 250 different Aboriginal languages. These groups were rather like the countries of Europe or the states of North America, but on a smaller scale. Every group had its own territory, politics and laws. The available water and the weather decided how many people could live off the land. Groups living in the more **fertile** country of south-east Australia had larger populations and occupied smaller areas of land.

The 250 different Aboriginal languages spoken throughout Australia were as different from each other as French is from Russian. There were also hundreds of **dialects**. Many Aboriginal people spoke several languages so that they could trade with neighbouring tribes. Complicated laws ruled the relationships Aboriginal people had with their families and with outsiders. These relationships were called 'kinship networks' and they guided the way people behaved every day.

A painting by Benjamin Duterreau of a Tasmanian Aborigine, 1838.

Tasmanian Aborigines

Aboriginal people arrived in Tasmania more than 25,000 years ago. Those at Kutakina Cave in the south-west lived further south than any other people in the world. They hunted wallabies, traded with other Aborigines, and travelled long distances to collect a mineral called ochre and stones for making tools. As the climate became warmer and wetter, rain forest completely covered the Kutakina area and the people left.

About 12,000 years ago the land joining Tasmania to the Australian mainland was covered by sea and Tasmania became an island. The Aborigines in Tasmania developed a new way of life and began to look different from the people on the mainland. Hunting weapons, such as boomerangs and spearthrowers, which were used in mainland Australia, were unknown in Tasmania.

Europeans forced Tasmanian Aborigines to live on mission stations (see page 40).

The Aborigines used their knowledge of the habits of animals to catch them. In Central Australia, they made emu traps by fixing the points of sharpened wooden stakes at the bottom of a large hole and covering the hole with branches. The emus walked over the branches and fell to their deaths on the spikes. Nets were used to catch fish, birds and larger animals, including sea mammals called **dugongs**. Complicated systems of channels, dams and pens were made out of stones, and fish and eels were swept along by the water currents into these traps. Poisons were used to stun fish, and sticky sap was spread on tree branches so that small birds would become stuck there.

These rocks are called The Pinnacles. *Aborigines believe that these rocks were created by ancestral spirit beings during the Dreamtime.*

Religious Land

Everything Aboriginal people did in their daily lives had both a practical and a religious purpose. This was because everything in their lives was related to the laws laid down during the Dreamtime (see page 7). These laws set out the religious duties that Aboriginal people had to perform on their land. The land was marked by the tracks of the ancestral spirit beings, who had left sacred sites behind them. Certain members of the group were made responsible for these sacred sites. During their religious ceremonies people sang and danced. Some tribes made paintings or decorated their bodies with feathers and ochre. Today, Aborigines who still follow a **semi-traditional** lifestyle continue to carry out these sacred duties to their land, and those who live in towns and cities still feel a bond with the lands of their people.

An artist's impression of Aborigines hunting with spears.

Aboriginal rock art of a kangaroo, found in Kakadu National Park in the Northern Territory.

Rock Art

Aboriginal artists have been painting and cutting pictures into rocks for thousands of years. The oldest rock paintings discovered so far are 30,000 years old. Rock pictures depict historical events such as images of the giant marsupials of long ago (see page 11), or the more recent arrival of European sailing ships (see below). They also show images of Dreamtime beings. These images are cared for and repainted in special ceremonies by Aborigines today.

There are spectacular cave galleries of paintings throughout Australia. Aboriginal artists used natural paints made from ochre, earth, bark and plants to make the colours red, yellow, black, brown and white. Styles of painting vary from place to place.

Trade and Exchange

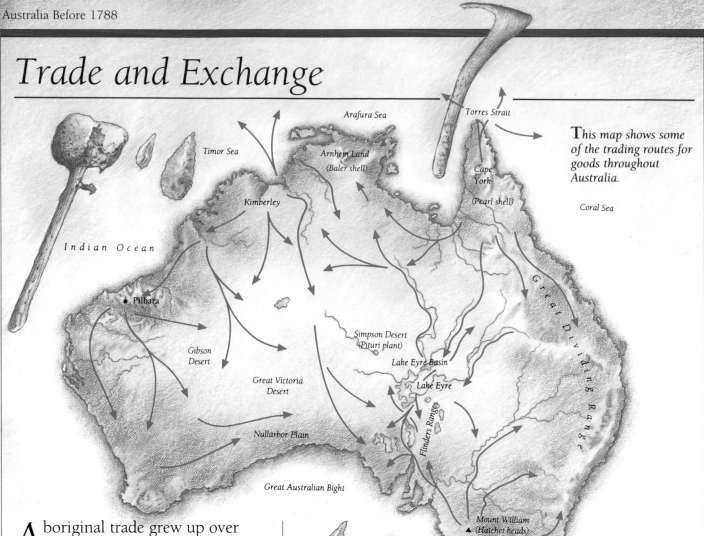

This map shows some of the trading routes for goods throughout Australia.

Arafura Sea
Torres Strait
Timor Sea
Arnhem Land
(Baler shell)
Cape York
(Pearl shell)
Coral Sea
Kimberley
Indian Ocean
Pilbara
Gibson Desert
Simpson Desert
(Pituri plant)
Great Victoria Desert
Lake Eyre Basin
Lake Eyre
Flinders Ranges
Great Dividing Range
Nullarbor Plain
Great Australian Bight
Mount William
(Hatchet heads)
Tasman Sea

Aboriginal trade grew up over thousands of years. Technology, music, art and stories were passed along trading routes from group to group. Gifts were exchanged between groups and sometimes goods were traded for goods of a similar value. This is called bartering and it was an important form of contact between Aboriginal people.

Sharing and Giving

In Aboriginal societies, sharing valuable items was an important part of social, political and religious life. When strangers met, they greeted each other by giving each other food or tools. Goods were exchanged to settle marriage arrangements and political or **legal** agreements. Songs, dances, stories and religious ideas were also exchanged between groups.

Hatchet stones

Trade Routes

Aboriginal trade routes criss-crossed Australia. These routes were made whenever groups met to perform ceremonies, share food and trade goods. Aborigines would travel several hundred kilometres to attend large meetings which were like trade markets. They travelled along traditional tracks laid down by the creator beings of the Dreamtime. These routes followed rivers and waterways and included 'safe' paths through the territory of rival groups.

As objects travelled further from their original homes, their uses changed. Away from the coast, pearl and baler shells were no longer everyday ornaments. For desert Aborigines, sections of shell became sacred objects. Aborigines in Arnhem Land used boomerangs made in Central Australia as musical sticks rather than as hunting tools.

Goods Travel Far

Baler shells

Raw materials (such as ochre, shells, stones and food) and crafts were traded throughout Australia. Goods that were common in one area were rare in another. For instance, greenstones used to make high-quality hatchet-heads were quarried at Mount William in Victoria. These hatchet-heads were sold or exchanged up to 800 kilometres away from Mount William. Hatchet-heads from quarries in Queensland were traded in Central Australia. Pearl shell from the north-west Kimberley coast has been found almost 2,000 kilometres inland! **Baler** shells from Cape York in Queensland and the Pilbara in Western Australia were also traded all over the continent.

Pearl shells

Trade at Early Sydney

When the British first settled at Sydney the Aborigines quickly adapted their own trading practices to meet the British demand for goods. The British needed food and wanted Aboriginal weapons to take to museums in Europe. The Aborigines wanted European iron and steel tools, hooks and fishing lines. The British were used to owning goods and private property and could not understand why the Aborigines wanted to share and exchange goods between friends, family and groups. This led to misunderstandings between Europeans and Aborigines.

A modern ironwood carving with cockatoo feathers by Declan Apuatimi

Ochre

The mineral called ochre (see picture right) was very important in Aboriginal life. It could be found in a variety of colours, including red and yellow. Aborigines used it to make a paint to decorate their bodies during ceremonies. They also used ochre to paint tools and rock art.

The Dieri People

The Dieri people lived in the dry country of the Lake Eyre Basin in Central Australia. During the winter, they camped in beehive-shaped huts along the river. Dieri trading parties travelled 500 kilometres south to trade with the owners of the Parachilna ochre mines near the Flinders Ranges. They exchanged boomerangs, spears and nets for ochre and grinding stones and performed special rituals and songs. When they returned to their camps, sometimes after two months, the traders were greeted with feasts.

In the autumn, the Dieri sometimes travelled 400 kilometres north to the edge of the Simpson Desert. They traded the ochre and grinding stones from the Flinders Ranges for pituri. This was a powerful drug made from the pituri bush. It was one of the most prized goods in Central Australia, and was traded across an area of half a million square kilometres. Hundreds of Aborigines gathered at pituri markets.

The Dieri obtained other goods from the southern and northern coasts through Aboriginal trading networks. These included hatchet stones, special woods to make shields, and objects made from baler and pearl shells.

This ochre mine in central western Australia was used as recently as 1939.

3 Visitors to Australia

European Voyages 1400s-1700s

No one knows when the first foreign visitors came to Australia. The spoken histories of the Aborigines of Arnhem Land tell of a mysterious people called the Baiini who visited in their sailing ships. Some historians believe that Chinese ships, commanded by the **Ming Dynasty** admiral Cheng Ho, visited Australia between 1405-33, although there is not much evidence to prove this. Small ships from eastern Indonesia may have been blown on to the Australian coastline. Historians know that fishermen from Macassar were visiting northern Australia regularly by the early 1700s (see page 25).

In Search of the 'South Land'

The ancient Greeks and Romans believed that the world was a sphere. In 150 CE the Greek geographer **Ptolemy** claimed that there must be a southern land to balance the northern land or the world would fall into the stars. Europeans continued to believe that the *Terra Australis*, or South Land, existed long after Ptolemy's death. They imagined that it was filled with gold, silver and spices.

From the fifteenth to the seventeenth centuries, the sea-going European powers competed with each other to explore the world's oceans and to find new trade routes and lands to add to their empires. The European discovery of 'new worlds' led to the establishment of **colonies** in the Americas, Africa and Asia.

This map of 1486 is based on the map in Ptolemy's book Geography.

Dutch Traders

During the seventeenth century the Dutch became the leading European traders in Asia. They had a trading base in Java and in 1606 Willem Jansz sailed from there in the *Duyfken*. He reached the western side of Cape York, where he had a violent meeting with the local Aborigines. The *Duyfken* was the first European ship in written history to reach Australia.

In 1611 a new and fast sailing route from the Cape of Good Hope to Java was discovered. But some ships were blown off course and as a result sighted the southern and western coasts of Australia. In 1616 Dirck Hartog's crew on the *Eendrach* landed at Shark Bay in Western Australia. Hartog hammered a pewter dish (see below) to a tree to mark this event. The dish was found 81 years later by another Dutch **navigator**, Willem de Vlamingh.

These are the remains of Dirck Hartog's pewter dish.

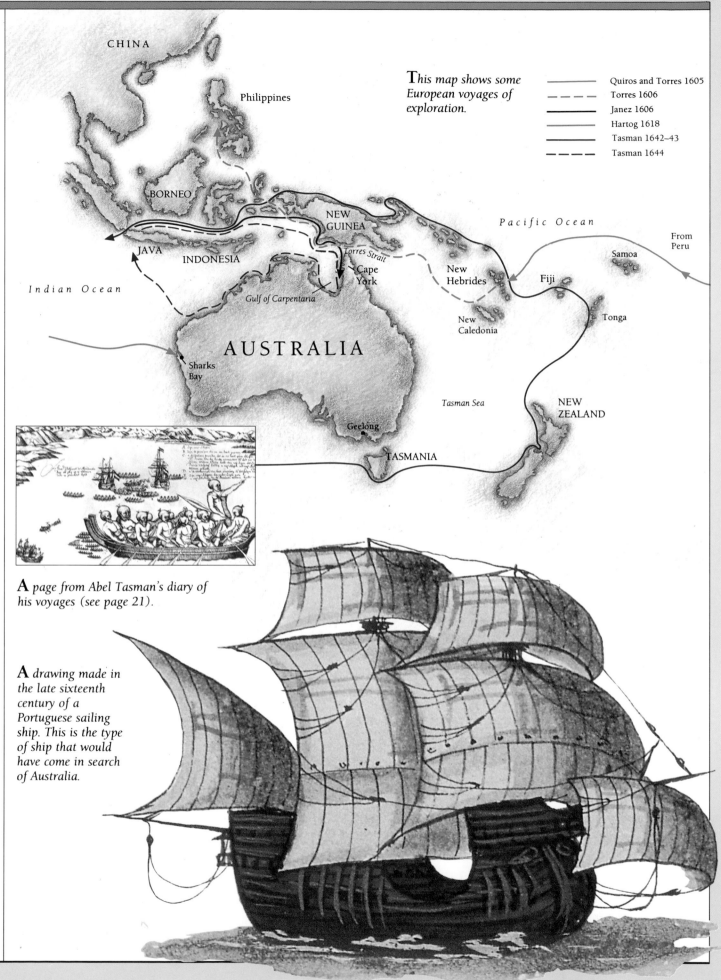

This map shows some European voyages of exploration.

Quiros and Torres 1605
Torres 1606
Janez 1606
Hartog 1618
Tasman 1642–43
Tasman 1644

CHINA

Philippines

BORNEO

NEW GUINEA

JAVA

INDONESIA

Indian Ocean

Torres Strait

Cape York

Gulf of Carpentaria

AUSTRALIA

Sharks Bay

Geelong

Tasman Sea

TASMANIA

Pacific Ocean

From Peru

Samoa

Fiji

New Hebrides

New Caledonia

Tonga

NEW ZEALAND

A page from Abel Tasman's diary of his voyages (see page 21).

A drawing made in the late sixteenth century of a Portuguese sailing ship. This is the type of ship that would have come in search of Australia.

The Portuguese Mystery – The Dieppe Maps

Between 1536 and 1566, cartographers (map makers) in the French town of Dieppe made a series of maps. These maps showed a southern continent discovered by the Portuguese which they called *Java-la-Grande*. The land was about the same size and in roughly the same place as the continent of Australia. But there is no mention of *Java-la-Grande* in any Portuguese records or maps dating from that time.

An *artist's impression of the Mahogany Ship being found in 1836.*

Keys and a Shipwreck

Some historians think that the Dieppe maps prove that the Portuguese visited Australia as early as 1522. Two mysterious objects found along the coastline of southern Australia may be further evidence of a Portuguese visit. In 1847, a bunch of keys was found buried near the shore at Geelong in Victoria. The Geelong Keys were described as 'old' and as the sort of keys that would fit the lock of a seaman's chest! But unfortunately the keys were lost.

In 1836, the wreck of a ship was found in the sandhills near Warnambool in Victoria. During the nineteenth century, many people saw the ship and described it as an old-fashioned vessel made of mahogany wood. These descriptions fit those of a sixteenth-century Portuguese ship. No one has seen the Mahogany Ship for 100 years. Was it covered by sand during a huge storm? Was it burnt for firewood? The Victorian state government recently offered a large reward to anyone who can solve the mystery. Modern-day treasure-seekers are searching the sandhills along the Victorian coast. If the Mahogany Ship is ever recovered, the riddle of the Dieppe maps and Portuguese visits to Australia may be answered.

The Portuguese and the Spaniards

The Portuguese dominated the trade routes between Europe and Asia during the sixteenth century and had a trading base in Timor. There is no written evidence that the Portuguese sailed south to Australia, but many people think that they must have explored this far.

From 1605 to 1607 Pedro Fernandez de Quiros led a Spanish expedition to find the South Land and teach its inhabitants Christianity. He thought he had found the South Land when he landed on an island in what is now called the New Hebrides. He named this *Austrialia del Espiritu Santo,* which means 'Southern Land of the Holy Spirit' in Spanish. One of his captains, Luis Vaez de Torres, sailed two ships through the narrow strait between Cape York and Papua New Guinea on his way to the Philippines. This is now called the Torres Strait, but no one knows whether Torres saw the Australian coast.

The *two Spanish ships commanded by Luis Vaez de Torres sailing through the Torres Strait.*

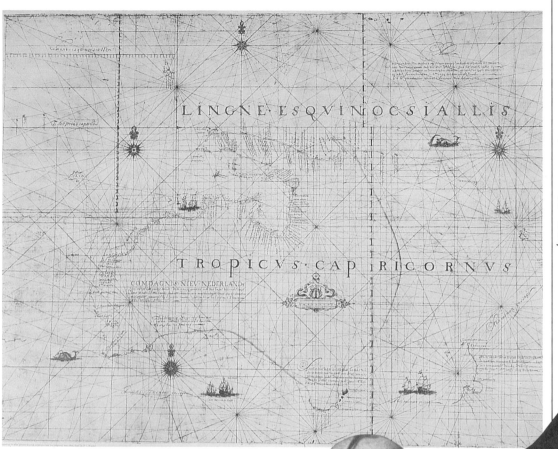

A map of Australia drawn by Abel Tasman in 1644.

A portrait of Abel Tasman, painted by the Dutch artist Jacob Cuyp.

The Expeditions of Abel Tasman

In 1642 and 1644 the **Dutch East India Company** sent Abel Tasman (1603-59) to look for trade opportunities in the South Land. Tasman navigated the coasts of the island that he named Van Diemen's Land (now Tasmania) and then sailed south to New Zealand. He also charted (mapped) the northern coast of the Australian mainland from his ship.

The Dutch mapped most of the coastline of Australia, which they called New Holland. But they were disappointed. The continent appeared to be either desert or dense rain forest. There were no signs of gold, spices or any other valuable items. After Tasman's voyages, there was no European exploration of Australia's coastlines for 126 years.

21

The British Explore the Pacific Ocean

The Voyage of the Endeavour

In 1768 the British **Admiralty** put the navigator and chart-maker Captain James Cook (1728-79) in command of the best-equipped scientific expedition ever. Cook's ship *Endeavour* went to Tahiti to study the planet Venus as it moved across the sun. From Tahiti, Cook was instructed to explore the South Pacific.

The *Endeavour* sailed to New Zealand and then to the east coast of Australia where a party landed at Botany Bay, near the site of the modern city of Sydney. The ship then sailed along the east coast and was damaged on the Great Barrier Reef. After repairs, Cook sailed around Cape York and landed on a small island he named Possession Island. Here, he claimed all the land he had seen for King George III and called it New South Wales.

Captain James Cook painted in 1775 by Nathaniel Dance.

Cook and the Aborigines

In his journal Cook described the Aborigines of eastern Australia as being *'far more happier than we Europeans'* because they lived in a society where everyone was equal and *'where all things necessary for life'* were provided by the earth and the sea. The Aborigines did not want *'magnificent houses of household stuff'* because they enjoyed the *'wholesome air'* of a *'warm and fine climate'*.

A painting by Willem van de Velde the Younger of Captain James Cook's ship the Resolution *in a storm.*

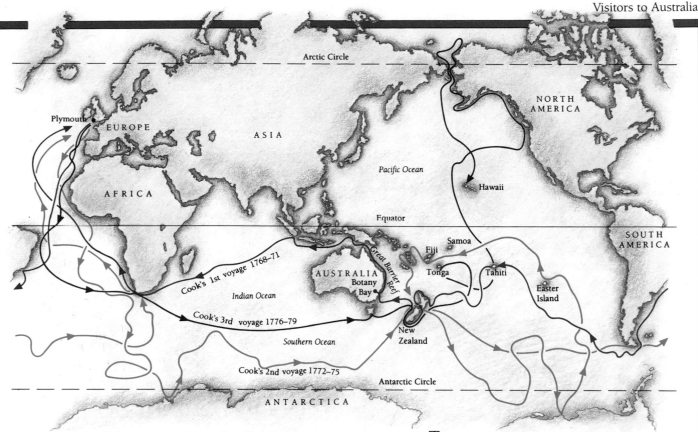

(Map labels:) Arctic Circle · NORTH AMERICA · Plymouth · EUROPE · ASIA · Pacific Ocean · Hawaii · AFRICA · Equator · SOUTH AMERICA · Samoa · Fiji · Cook's 1st voyage 1768–71 · AUSTRALIA · Botany Bay · Great Barrier Reef · Tonga · Tahiti · Indian Ocean · Easter Island · Cook's 3rd voyage 1776–79 · Southern Ocean · New Zealand · Cook's 2nd voyage 1772–75 · Antarctic Circle · ANTARCTICA

Cook's Second and Third Voyages

Cook commanded the *Resolution* on his second and most important voyage of exploration in 1772-5. This voyage proved that the land he had named New South Wales was the only continent in the southern hemisphere. Cook was the first navigator to travel around the world from west to east and the first to enter the Antarctic Circle. On a third voyage from 1776 to 1779, Cook explored the islands of Hawaii and sailed north to the Arctic Circle. Cook returned to Hawaii in 1779, and was killed there during a fight between the Hawaiians and his crew.

Captain Cook was killed when a fight broke out between his crew and the Hawaiians. This is how the artist J. Clevely imagined that Cook died.

This map shows the routes of Cook's three voyages of exploration.

A *portrait of William Dampier.*

Pirates Explore Australia First!

The English adventurer William Dampier (c. 1650-1715) spent three months in Australia in 1688. He was a crew member on the pirate ship *Cygnet*. The pirates landed on the north-west coast of Australia so that they could make repairs to their ship. Dampier later returned to England where he wrote a book about his experiences called *A New Voyage Around the World*.

Joseph Banks named this common Australian plant the Banksia serrata *after himself.*

Scientists in the Pacific

The British began to explore the Pacific Ocean in search of trade in the 1760s. European maps of the Pacific were incomplete and the South Land was still a mystery.

During the eighteenth century there was a new interest in Europe in **natural science**. The British explored the Pacific to discover more about nature and to collect and record all forms of life, from butterflies and bees to palm trees and volcanoes. Plants, animals and sometimes people were taken back to Britain to be examined by scientists and displayed in museums.

This portrait of Joseph Banks was painted by Thomas Phillips when Banks was president of the Royal Society.

Circumnavigating the Continent

Gradually, British maps of the Australian coast were completed. The navigator Matthew Flinders (1774-1814) **surveyed** the southern and eastern coastlines, and was the first person to **circumnavigate** the continent between 1802 and 1803. On his way back to England, Flinders stopped at the French island of Mauritius. Here he was thrown into prison because France and Britain were at war. During his six years in prison, Flinders wrote about his Australian expedition. He was finally released in 1810 and his important book *A Voyage to Terra Australis* was published in 1814 – a day before he died from ill-health. Flinders' maps of Australia were so accurate they were still used 50 years after his death.

This is a picture of the First Fleet landing at Botany Bay in 1788. The picture is dated 1789 and includes one of the first images of an Aborigine seen by British people.

Joseph Banks and Botany Bay

The young **botanist** Joseph Banks (1744-1820) accompanied Cook on the *Endeavour*, and collected 3,600 plant and animal specimens on the voyage – 1,400 of which were new to Europeans. Cook named the place where the *Endeavour* first landed Botany Bay because Banks gathered so many plants there.

In 1778, Banks was elected president of the **Royal Society** and became very influential. He recommended Botany Bay as the ideal place for a **convict** settlement. In 1788, the First Fleet of convicts landed at Botany Bay but could not find enough drinking water to support a settlement. So they moved nine kilometres north and began building the town of Sydney.

The Macassans in Northern Australia

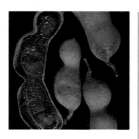

These are the seeds of tamarind trees. They have been found at old Macassan camps and prove that the Macassans brought this fruit to Australia.

A number of Aborigines journeyed to Macassar with the trepang collectors and a few travelled as far as Singapore.

The Macassan praus (below) which sailed to northern Australia have not been used in Sulawesi for at least 50 years. In the 1980s the Macassan voyages to Australia were recreated. A prau was built and named the Hati Marege. It sailed from Sulawesi to Australia during the wet season of 1987-88.

From the 1700s, and possibly earlier, the coasts of northern Australia were visited regularly by fleets of dug-out sailing canoes called praus. These came from Macassar in Sulawesi, now in modern-day Indonesia. The crews of the praus have become known as Macassans.

The Macassans' canoes took about ten days to reach Australia. Probably between 20 to 60 praus sailed every year to Arnhem Land in Australia's Northern Territory. Each prau carried about 40 crew members. Smaller fleets also visited the Kimberley coastline of Western Australia.

Trepang Fisheries

The Macassans came to collect trepang. Trepang are sea creatures also known as sea-cucumbers. They burrow at the bottom of reefs and can be up to 60 centimetres long.

Trepang were Australia's first **export**. The Macassans sold them to the Chinese, who believed that they were delicacies with healing powers. The Macassans gathered about 350 tonnes of trepang every year.

Trepang were collected by hand in shallow water or by diving from small canoes in deeper water. They were then boiled in huge iron pots before being dried in the sun and smoked on bamboo racks.

Friendly Traders

Macassan crews worked together setting up camps that protected them from Aboriginal attacks. But relations between the two peoples were mostly friendly. The Aborigines on the coast became used to the regular visits of the Macassans. Aborigines started to use Macassan words, wrote songs and performed dances and ceremonies about their visitors. They painted pictures of the praus and copied their design.

4 White People Invade

Penal Colonies and Free Immigrants

The British claimed that under English law Australia was *terra nullius* or unoccupied. This means that the British did not recognize the fact that Aborigines already lived there. Instead, the British argued that they were the first people to claim Australia and had the right to settle there. From an Aboriginal point of view, the British were invaders.

Convicts in Exile

In January 1788, the First Fleet arrived at Botany Bay from England after a journey of eight months. A few government officers and several hundred convicts came ashore to build the **penal colony** of New South Wales. Over the next 80 years, about 137,000 men and 25,000 women were transported to Australia. The majority of these convicts had been very poor in Britain and had stolen food or other small items. For this they were transported to Australia with an average sentence of seven years hard labour (enforced work). Most convicts had to work for people who had gone to Australia of their own free will (called free settlers). If the convicts misbehaved they were chained together and made to work on road-gangs. The transportation of convicts to New South Wales and Tasmania was abolished in the 1840s. In Western Australia transportation began in 1850 and did not stop until 1868.

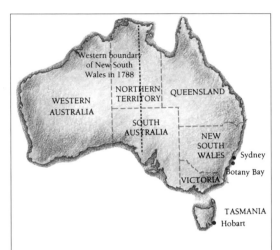

Dividing the Continent

The British divided Australia into separate areas of land, called colonies. Each colony had its own government. The map above shows the boundaries of the colonies in 1911. Colonies' boundaries frequently changed before 1911.

A *painting of 1853 shows an immigrant family on their way to the goldfields. You can see mining equipment such as shovels, picks and gold-pans among their belongings.*

Free Immigration

During the early nineteenth century, unemployment and poverty increased in Britain. The British government wanted to send the poor to the Australian colonies. The Australian colonies needed male labourers to clear and farm the land and single women to work as servants and marry the labourers. So between 1830 and 1850 the British government agreed to assist people by paying their travelling expenses to Australia. After the discovery of gold in the early 1850s, there was no shortage of immigrants travelling south to seek their fortunes.

The Journey South

On the transportation ships, convicts were crammed below deck and allowed on deck for fresh air only once a day. The conditions were not much better for poor or 'assisted' immigrants. They were packed into large dormitories (sleeping areas) on the lower decks of the ship. These were lined with bunks and had a dining table down the middle. In this crowded, airless space disease spread quickly.

A cartoon of convicts outside Sydney jail in 1800.

A painting of 1823 (left) of the harbour of Port Jackson and the country between the city of Sydney and the Blue Mountains of New South Wales.

Caroline Chisholm on board a ship bound for Australia.

Caroline Chisholm

When Caroline Chisholm (1808-77) came to Sydney from England in 1838, she was shocked that the government gave no help to female immigrants when they first arrived. Many women were unable to find jobs or places to stay and had no choice but to live on the streets. Caroline Chisholm set up a hostel, or home, for newly-arrived women. She also helped at least 11,000 immigrants find jobs and homes.

In colonial Australia, men greatly outnumbered women. Caroline Chisholm believed that women and children were needed to make society civilized and so she encouraged British families to emigrate to Australia.

Convicts caged below deck on their way to Australia.

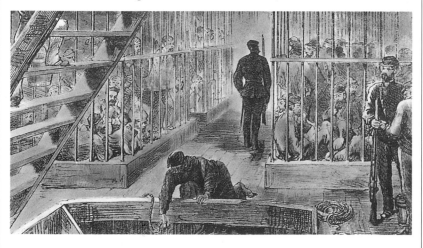

Opening Up the Land

In 1901, the nation of Australia was formed when the colonies joined together under a national government. By this time, most of the land in Australia had been taken by white settlers for agriculture and mining. Land was needed to provide food and raw materials for the new settlers and to supply British trade. By the 1830s wool was Australia's most valuable export. Later in the century meat, wheat and gold also became important exports.

Squatters and Selectors

The colonial governments sold, leased (rented) and gave land to settlers, although some settlers made their own rules. From the 1820s wealthy pastoralists (farmers who used the land for grazing animals), known as squatters, began occupying large areas of land. They moved in their cattle and sheep and built fences and homes. They were often the first Europeans to enter a region and were followed by shopkeepers, tradespeople, and colonial officials such as the police.

By the mid 1800s, schemes were introduced to help more people to select small areas of farming land. But many of the farms taken up by these people, called selectors, failed because the land was poor and European farming methods didn't work on Australian soil in Australia's climate.

Stock Routes

Throughout the nineteenth century, more and more grazing land was claimed by pastoralists. Sheep and cattle (called stock) had to be herded on to these lands, and then on to the markets in the capital cities of the south-east. Thousands of kilometres of stock routes soon criss-crossed the continent (see above).

The workers who moved the stock were called drovers. It could take several months for the drovers and their dogs to take the stock to market. One of the longest stock routes ran from Katherine in the Northern Territory, south to Alice Springs and on to Adelaide on the coast.

Gold

In 1851, gold was discovered at Ophir in New South Wales. Within days, 2,000 miners had rushed there to begin digging. Other gold fields were opened in Victoria during the 1850s, in Queensland during the 1860s, in the Northern Territory during the 1880s, and in Western Australia during the 1890s.

The discovery of gold had an enormous impact. By the end of 1851, half of the adult men in Victoria were working on the gold fields. The gold-miners were known as prospectors. As hundreds of thousands of people poured in, the colonial population became three times larger in only ten years. Large mining towns sprang up, and in the capital cities grand buildings were constructed with the money made from gold-mining.

Only a few miners became rich. The merchants and shopkeepers were the ones who really made their fortunes. Most miners abandoned the gold fields after a few years. But some travelled from the gold fields of Victoria and New South Wales to the new gold-mines in north and west Australia. Prospectors roamed through the outback (the interior of Australia), always looking for a gold nugget – and they continue to do so today.

This nineteenth-century painting (left) of cattle droving in New South Wales is by the Australian artist S. T. Gill.

A mining scene from the Australian gold fields.

On the Track

More workers were needed on stations and farms at particular times of the year to cope with harvesting, **shearing** and fruit picking. Many workers travelled through the country looking for this work. The wool industry depended on shearers who went from farm to farm cutting sheep's fleeces. Australian writers and painters have created many myths about these workers, called bushmen.

When unemployment was high, thousands of poor Australians would leave the cities and towns with their belongings in a 'swag' (bag) and go 'on the track'. This happened during the depressions of the 1890s and the 1930s. Men, and some women and children, travelled on foot, on horseback and in wagons through the country, hoping to find work and trying to live off the land.

Men on the track play cards in 1878. One man is leaning on his swag.

Chinese and Melanesian Workers

People who came to Australia from places outside Europe had to adjust to a totally different way of life. The Australian colonies were part of the British Empire and white settlers thought that they were better than coloured people. When the new Australian **federal** parliament was formed in 1901, the first legislation they passed was the White Australia Policy. This limited the number of non-white immigrants who could come to Australia. But white settlers also believed that non-white people could be used as cheap labour on the sugar cane plantations in north Queensland.

The Chinese in Australia

In the 1840s, British settlers brought Chinese people to the colonies to work on farms. Chinese immigration increased dramatically with the discovery of gold in the 1850s. By 1857 there were 25,000 Chinese people in Victoria alone. On some gold fields the Chinese outnumbered Europeans by seven to one.

This is a photograph of a Chinese funeral in an Australian town around 1900.

By the 1880s, the Chinese population in Australia had reached 40,000.

The Great Gold Mountain

Chinese miners began their journey to Australia – which they called the 'great gold mountain' – from farming villages in southern China. Almost all the immigrants were men whose fares were paid by wealthy Chinese merchants. To repay this debt they had to work for one year without wages. Any gold found during this time belonged to the merchants.

Fights broke out on the gold fields between white miners and Chinese miners. This drawing by S. T. Gill was made in 1856.

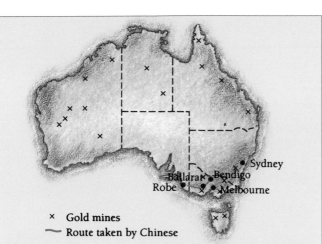

The Chinese miners walked along this route to the gold fields of Victoria.

Map legend:
× Gold mines
— Route taken by Chinese

Locations shown: Sydney, Ballarat, Bendigo, Robe, Melbourne

Walking to the Goldfields

White colonists did not welcome the Chinese on the gold fields. Riots broke out and some Chinese miners were killed. In 1855, the Victorian government introduced a new tax on every Chinese immigrant. To avoid the tax, ships would unload their Chinese passengers along the South Australian coast. From here, the Chinese walked for hundreds of kilometres through desert and bushland to reach the Victorian gold fields. This was a dangerous and difficult journey and many people died on the way.

Chinese tents and public notices like these reconstructions would have been a common sight on the Australian gold fields.

Labour from the Pacific Islands

In north Queensland, white settlers wanted a large and cheap labour force to work on the farms and sugar cane plantations. So from the 1860s, about 60,000 Melanesian workers were brought from islands in the Pacific, mainly the Solomons and the New Hebrides. Many were kidnapped or tricked into going to Australia, but others agreed to go.

Life in the Canefields

The Melanesians were given a contract to work for a small wage for a minimum of three years. After that, they could choose to return to their islands or continue working in Australia. Although they were legally free, they worked and lived like slaves. Work in the canefields was hard and the housing and food provided by the plantation owners was often bad. Thousands of Melanesians died from disease and exhaustion.

The End of Forced Labour

The Australian government stopped the use of labour from the Pacific Islands after 1904. Many Melanesians did not want to leave Australia, which they regarded as their home, but most were forced to go back to the islands where they were born.

Melanesian workers unload and stack sugar cane on a Queensland planation.

5 European Exploration

Exploring the Interior

Charles Sturt surveying the desert in 1829.

From 1788, when the first penal settlement was established at Sydney, the British began exploring Australia in search of farming and grazing land. During the 1800s, expeditions set off from the various new cities and towns on the coastline. But the dense forests of the south-east, the lack of rivers and water-holes, and the vast stretches of desert made the interior of the continent difficult to explore.

The Explorers

The first European explorers were military officers. They were soon followed by groups of trained surveyors, scientists and adventurers sent by governments and private companies. However, pastoralists in search of land and prospectors seeking minerals were often the first white people to travel through remote parts of Australia.

Rivers Flowing Inland

After the Blue Mountains (west of Sydney) were crossed in 1813 by William Lawson, Gregory Blaxland and William Charles Wentworth, the exploration of south-east Australia began. The discovery that the Lachlan and Macquarie rivers flowed to the west – that is inland – convinced many people that there must be a sea in the middle of Australia. In 1817, the Englishman John Oxley (1783-1828) reported that the Lachlan and Macquarie rivers ended in marshes, and suggested that they were on the edge of an inland sea.

A portrait of Charles Sturt.

The Inland Sea

The search for the inland sea was the main aim of Australian exploration for several years. In 1827 the British explorer Charles Sturt (1795-1869) discovered the Darling River. The next year, he sailed down the Murrumbidgee River to the mouth of the Murray, Australia's largest river.

Sturt's expedition proved that most of the eastern half of Australia drained into the Murray-Darling river system. This explained why the rivers flowed west, but people still believed in an inland sea. Edward John Eyre (1815-1901) led three expeditions north from Adelaide between 1839 and 1841 to look for the imaginary sea. After finding Lake Torrens, he thought that the sea was part of a huge horseshoe-shaped lake blocking the way north.

Crossing East to West

After failing to travel around his imagined lake, Eyre headed west into the desert with a white companion and three Aboriginal guides. The party was attacked by local Aborigines, and only Eyre and one Aboriginal guide, Wylie, survived. Together they continued west along the shores of the **Great Australian Bight**. Eyre was dependent on Wylie's survival skills during the gruelling months it took to reach the western Australian coast. By the end of the journey Eyre had become the first European to cross the western half of Australia.

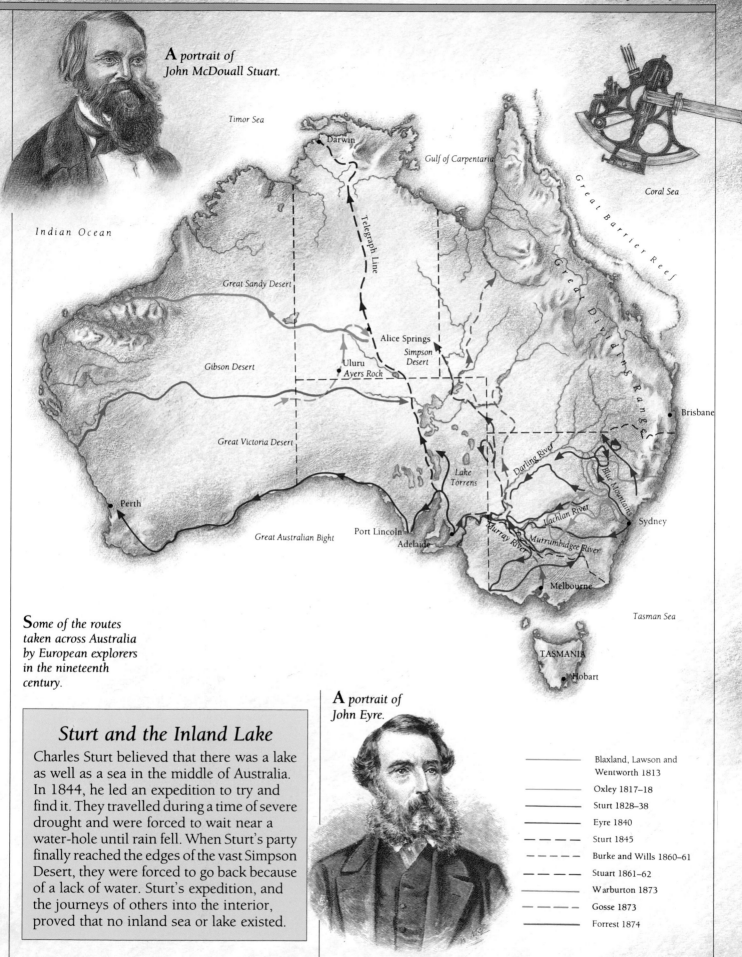

A portrait of
John McDouall Stuart.

Timor Sea

Darwin

Gulf of Carpentaria

Coral Sea

Indian Ocean

Telegraph Line

Great Sandy Desert

Great Barrier Reef

Great Dividing Range

Alice Springs

Simpson Desert

Gibson Desert

Uluru
Ayers Rock

Brisbane

Great Victoria Desert

Lake
Torrens

Darling River

Blue Mountains

Perth

Lachlan River

Sydney

Great Australian Bight

Port Lincoln

Murray River

Murrumbidgee River

Adelaide

Melbourne

Tasman Sea

Some of the routes
taken across Australia
by European explorers
in the nineteenth
century.

TASMANIA

Hobart

Sturt and the Inland Lake

Charles Sturt believed that there was a lake
as well as a sea in the middle of Australia.
In 1844, he led an expedition to try and
find it. They travelled during a time of severe
drought and were forced to wait near a
water-hole until rain fell. When Sturt's party
finally reached the edges of the vast Simpson
Desert, they were forced to go back because
of a lack of water. Sturt's expedition, and
the journeys of others into the interior,
proved that no inland sea or lake existed.

A portrait of
John Eyre.

————	Blaxland, Lawson and Wentworth 1813
————	Oxley 1817–18
————	Sturt 1828–38
————	Eyre 1840
– – – –	Sturt 1845
- - - -	Burke and Wills 1860–61
— — —	Stuart 1861–62
————	Warburton 1873
– – – –	Gosse 1873
————	Forrest 1874

The Race to Cross the Continent

By the early 1850s, Europeans had mapped much of Australia and its good farming land. But soon explorers were competing to cross the continent in one journey.

In 1860 an Irish ex-police officer, Robert O'Hara Burke (1820-61), left Melbourne with an expedition of 17 men, enough food for several months, camels, horses and wagons piled with firewood. Burke was so impatient that he left most of his expedition members at different points (called depots) on the way. From his second depot at Merindie, Burke headed north with his second-in-command, the Englishman John Wills (1834-61), two men named King and Gray, and some camels and provisions. The camels died, but the men reached the Gulf of Carpentaria, and so became the first Europeans to cross Australia from north to south. They took weeks to walk back to the Coopers Creek depot, and Gray died on the journey. When the others reached it, exhausted and starving, they found that the depot had been abandoned only hours earlier. Local Aborigines offered them food, but Burke shot at them. He and Wills died, but King survived because he accepted Aboriginal help.

A *portrait of Robert O'Hara Burke.*

Burke and Wills *make their way across the desert.*

A *portrait of John Wills.*

A *carving on a tree at the Coopers Creek depot of Robert O'Hara Burke.*

The dead Robert O'Hara Burke, with King by his side.

Afghan immigrants brought camels to central Australia in the 1860s. Known as 'ships of the desert', the camels were used to carry goods.

The Scotsman John McDouall Stuart (1815-66) also dreamed of crossing the continent. He made two failed attempts, driven back by Aboriginal attacks and the harsh conditions. From 1861 to 1862, Stuart succeeded in travelling from Adelaide to Arnhem Land through the geographical centre of the continent.

West of the Centre

The final European explorations of Australia were into the desert west of the Overland Telegraph Line. The telegraph line was completed in 1872 and followed Stuart's route through Central Australia. In 1873 the German, William Gosse (1842-81) left the telegraph station at Alice Springs and came upon Uluru (Ayers Rock), a massive dome-shaped rock over three kilometres long. The same year, Peter Warburton (1813-89) led an expedition west from Alice Springs across the Great Sandy Desert. John Forrest (1847-1918) travelled from the western Australian coast across the desert to the telegraph line in 1874, while Ernest Giles (1835-97) used camels as pack animals to travel west from the Telegraph Line to Perth in 1875. All these expeditions confirmed that the centre of Australia was dominated by huge deserts.

The **Prussian** explorer and **naturalist** Ludwig Leichhardt (1813-48) arrived in Sydney in 1842 to explore Australia. He travelled from southern Queensland to Port Essington on the Gulf of Carpentaria. He then made two attempts to cross the continent from east to west, from Queensland to Western Australia. On the second attempt in 1848, he disappeared without trace in the interior.

Paul Edmund Strzelecki (1797-1873) was a Polish explorer who arrived in Sydney in 1839. He explored Tasmania and New South Wales, crossed the Australian Alps, and mapped much of eastern Victoria. When he returned to Europe in 1843 he published several books about his travels.

Aboriginal Guides

Expeditions often relied on the knowledge of Aborigines to guide them and find food and water. But these Aboriginal guides did not receive the recognition or the rewards given to white explorers. Some explorers, such as Thomas Mitchell (1792-1855), a Scot who was famous for surveying south-eastern Australia, murdered and ill-treated Aborigines. In several instances, Aborigines attacked expeditions, but on other occasions they saved explorers from dying.

Transcontinental Links

As European settlements spread across Australia the demand for roads and communication services increased. Making roads and laying railways was hard work. The first roads were built by convicts, and Chinese labourers constructed the railway in the Northern Territory. The workers who laid the Overland Telegraph Line in 1870-72 toiled across thousands of miles of dry, hot land that had been unexplored by Europeans only a decade before. All these people were, in different ways, explorers far from home.

River Transport

After Europeans discovered the great Murray River and its **tributaries**, towns and pastoral stations were set up in the Murray region. The quickest and cheapest form of travel between these settlements was by boat along rivers. During the 1880s, barges and paddle-steamers travelled thousands of kilometres through the waterways of the Murray-Darling region.

Supplies being unloaded on the Murray River in the 1860s.

The viaduct on Hills railway in South Australia.

Rail Links

By the 1870s railways were being built for the new mining and pastoral towns. In the Murray region, the railways gradually took over from the paddle-steamers. Railway tracks from the capital cities and the coast ran into the interior in a vast system. Eventually, the east coast from Sydney to Cairns was joined by rail, Adelaide was linked to Alice Springs, and a railway was built from Adelaide across the Nullarbor Plain to Perth.

Roads Replace Rail

When cars became cheaper in the 1950s, roads began to replace railways as a cheap and efficient way of transporting people and goods. A network of national motorways was built and roads were upgraded. Today roads are the most important transport routes throughout Australia.

Planting the first pole of the Overland Telegraph on 15 September 1870.

The Overland Telegraph

In 1872 the Overland Telegraph was completed, connecting Australia with overseas telegraph networks for the first time. More than 3,000 kilometres of telegraph lines and poles were built from the South Australian coast through the centre of the continent to Darwin.

From Darwin, the line went via submarine cable to Indonesia and then through Singapore, Malaysia, India, Egypt and Europe to Britain. In just a few hours, a message in Morse code could be sent over 20,000 kilometres. This was amazingly fast at a time when it took weeks to travel from Britain by ship. At each telegraph post, an operator would receive the message and then tap it on to the next post. The telegraph system brought Australia into close contact with international trade and banking and had a significant effect on the economy.

The first Australians to fly from Britain to Australia, 1919.

Air Travel

Australia's vast size makes air travel very important. Early pilots tested many new planes in Australia. The most famous was Charles Kingsford Smith (1897-1935) who set the world records for crossing Australia by air and for flying from America to Australia.

Airlines began offering services throughout Australia during the 1920s, and international services by the 1930s. Then, it took just over 12 days to fly to London. Only wealthy people could afford to travel by air before the 1960s.

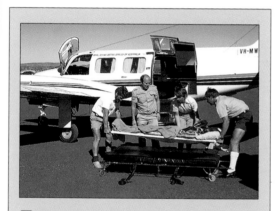

The modern-day Flying Doctor Service takes essential medical help to people living in the outback.

The Flying Doctor Service

Air travel and communication networks have changed the lives of isolated Australian communities. Small planes and helicopters are now used on cattle and sheep farms to round up stock and check fences. The Flying Doctor Service operates medical and ambulance services from its fleet of aeroplanes. It also gives medical advice over the radio, and provides the radio facilities for the School of the Air – a school for pupils who live in isolated places. This educational service is unique to Australia and involves teachers and students communicating by radio over thousands of kilometres.

6 Fighting Back

Frontier Wars

Europeans landed in Australia at many different points on the coast and so there were lots of places where Europeans and Aborigines met for the first time. European exploration took place over a long period of time and under many different circumstances. For coastal Aborigines the arrival of Europeans from the sea was totally unexpected. But news of the whites, their animals and their guns, travelled quickly into the interior. Once the Aborigines realized that the Europeans intended to stay and take their lands war broke out all over Australia.

Open War

The Aborigines resisted European settlers by fighting battles with them and also through **guerrilla warfare**. Groups of Aborigines made surprise attacks on settlers and their sheep and cattle, and then disappeared into the bush. At first, Aboriginal spears and fighting skills could match the slow-loading guns of the settlers. But by the 1860s the colonists were using rifles and revolvers which didn't need loading as often and this gave them an advantage. The frontier was a violent place. The Europeans attacked Aboriginal men and women, kidnapped children and murdered entire groups. In 1838 seven white men were

sentenced to death for killing 28 Aborigines at Myall Creek in New South Wales, but this was very unusual. The government and its courts rarely punished Europeans for murdering or mistreating Aborigines.

Aboriginal armed resistance was so strong that it delayed the settlement of some areas of Australia for several years. In Queensland alone, at least 1,000 settlers and 10,000 Aborigines were killed fighting. European **massacres** of Aborigines and Aboriginal armed resistance to invasion continued until the 1930s in parts of the Northern Territory.

*A*borigines sometimes set fire to the land to force European settlers and their stock to leave (above left). This picture was painted in 1836.

*D*uring this expedition to the Torres Strait in 1842, some European explorers were threatened by Aborigines.

By 1890, many Aboriginal people had to rely on the government for food.

Disease and Starvation

European diseases such as smallpox, influenza, measles and even the common cold were deadly for Aboriginal populations, who had no **immunity** to them. Smallpox almost wiped out many Aboriginal groups in the early 1800s. Influenza and measles killed large numbers of people in Central Australia as recently as the 1950s. As Aborigines were driven from their lands and their food supplies, some died of starvation. From an original Aboriginal population of three million in 1788, only 50,000 were left in 1900.

Pemulwuy

Pemulwuy (died 1802) was a famous Aboriginal guerrilla leader. His peoples' lands lay around Botany Bay, near Sydney. Between 1790 and 1802, Pemulwuy led attacks on British settlers and destroyed their crops. After a raid on the settlement at Parramatta in 1797, the British offered a reward for his capture or death. Pemulwuy was shot in a police ambush. The Governor of New South Wales sent his head to England as a scientific specimen. Pemulwuy's son, Tedbury, succeeded him in waging guerrilla warfare against the British, but he was captured and imprisoned in 1805.

Europeans driving Aborigines from their lands.

The Tasmanian Aborigines

Europeans settled in Tasmania in 1803 and the first massacre of Aborigines occurred a year later. In the 1820s more settlers arrived and the Aborigines attacked them and their animals. In 1828 the Governor of Tasmania declared war on the Aborigines, giving settlers permission to shoot them on sight.

In 1830 settlers made a human chain called the Black Line. In this chain they moved across the island, driving Aborigines out of the settled lands. Then, George Augustus Robinson (1788-1866) was appointed by the Tasmanian government to make contact with the Aborigines that were left and capture them. Robinson gathered the remaining 135 Aborigines and took them to Flinders Island. In 1847 the 47 survivors of this group were sent back to Tasmania. The last of these survivors, a woman named Truganini, died in 1876. From that time, whites have called Truganini the 'last of the Tasmanians'. Many people still believe that Tasmanian Aborigines are extinct, but Aboriginal communities had been founded on the islands of the Bass Strait. Today, Tasmanian Aborigines are fighting for recognition and rights to their traditional lands.

Some Aborigines were persuaded to join a Native Police force which was used to drive out other Aborigines from rival groups.

Aboriginal Resistance

A *famous painting of 1840 by Benjamin Duterrau entitled* The Conciliation. *The painting shows George Augustus Robinson with Tasmanian Aborigines (see box on page 39).*

The British tried to make the Aborigines follow a European way of life. The Aborigines were forced to settle down, become farmers, forget their religious beliefs and become Christians. During the nineteenth century, white people predicted that Aboriginal peoples would become extinct. However, Aboriginal resistance to European society was too strong for this to happen and early this century Aborigines began growing in numbers.

Missions, Reserves and Farms

Colonial governments set aside land where Aborigines were forced to live. These areas were called reserves and were run by the government. Aborigines were also forced to live on **mission stations** controlled by Christian **missionaries**. The missionaries tried to make Aboriginal people give up their beliefs and religious ceremonies. The government gradually sold a lot of the reserve land to white farmers, so the Aborigines were left to live in camps on the edges of towns.

Government Policies

By 1911, all the Australian states had passed Protection Acts which set out how Aborigines could live. In some states, Aborigines needed permission to move around the country or even to get married. They could not own property and were often forced to work for no wages.

One government policy took thousands of Aboriginal children (particularly those with non-Aboriginal fathers) away from their mothers. The government believed that if the children were brought up away from their families they would fit into white society more successfully.

Modern-day Aborigines from the Walpiri group in the Tanimi Desert.

Aboriginal People Today

There are now about 270,000 Aborigines and Torres Strait Islanders in Australia and they mostly live in country towns or cities. They still have to cope with the problems brought about by the loss of their lands and being forced to live in a white society. Many Aborigines live in poverty, with limited access to health care and schools. Aboriginal communities have many more unemployed people, child deaths and people in prison than white communities. Aborigines also have to fight against the racism of some white Australians. In 1988, Aborigines protested against 200 years of white invasion. But today their future is more secure than it has been since 1788 because they are gradually getting more rights to health care and education. Aboriginal people are becoming involved in many more areas of the Australian economy and white Australians are learning more about Aboriginal culture.

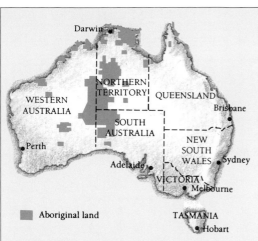

The shaded areas on the map show land owned by Aborigines (1988).

Gaining Rights

Aborigines have been campaigning for legal and social rights since the 1930s. After the Second World War, Aboriginal cattle workers in northern Australia went on strike to demand better conditions, but they were not paid the same as white workers until 1965. In 1967, Australians voted to give Aborigines full citizenship. Since then, Aborigines have continued to fight for the right to govern themselves. They have set up their own health, legal and housing services, and government spending on Aborigines has increased.

Aborigines have demanded land rights – the right to control their old lands – for many years. In the 1970s and 1980s, new laws gave some Aborigines some control of their lands and sacred sites. But this issue remains a very controversial one in Australia. Mining companies have protested against Aborigine land rights because they fear it might stop them from mining in certain areas.

Family ties are of great importance for today's Aborigines.

Journeys to a New Land

Australians volunteered to fight for Britain in World War I. More than 60,000 men were killed. This painting by George Lambert shows Australian troops at Gallipoli in April 1915.

Apart from the Aborigines, all Australians travelled to Australia in recent history from other places. In the first half of the twentieth century, Australia was often described as the continent with 'the most room for more people'. In the 1920s there were ambitious plans for 50 or 100 million more immigrants to fill the empty spaces in Australia's centre. After the Second World War (1939-45) immigration to Australia from countries other than Britain increased on a massive scale and transformed Australia completely.

Recent Explorers

In the 1940s, 98 per cent of Australia's seven million people were originally British. But Britain could no longer supply enough new immigrants for Australia, so immigrants were taken from other European countries. Many of these people had lost their homes during the war in Europe and wanted to start a new life. Some of these people were able to pay their own fares, but the Australian government helped others. In return, 'assisted' immigrants agreed to work for the government for two years.

Between 1947 and 1971, almost three million people travelled to Australia from Britain, the Netherlands, Germany, Italy, Greece, the Middle East and other countries. In 1973, the White Australia Policy was replaced with a policy that did not discriminate against immigrants on racial grounds. Immigration from

A ship bringing immigrants to Australia in the early 1900s.

South East Asia increased dramatically in the 1970s, with refugees coming from Cambodia, Laos and Vietnam. Thousands of Vietnamese refugees travelled more than 11,000 kilometres from Asia in small, flimsy boats to Australia's northern coasts. Today, about a quarter of all Australians were born overseas in more than 100 different countries. Although immigrants are still coming to Australia, the rate of immigration is now strictly controlled.

A Multicultural Society

At first, immigrants from non-British backgrounds were expected to blend into Australian society. They were not encouraged to speak their own languages or keep their customs. They were also seen as a cheap labour force to do the jobs Australians wouldn't do. But these immigrant communities soon set up their own organizations, schools and newspapers and began to demand special services from the government. During the 1970s, the government introduced a policy of multiculturism. The government now recognizes and supports different cultures, rather than trying to make everyone behave in the same way. Modern-day Australia is an exciting mixture of different cultures, where people of many different origins live together without much tension.

By the year 2030, it is estimated that one-third of Australia's population will be of Asian origin. This photograph (left) shows Chinatown in the city of Melbourne.

Australians today in the city of Melbourne.

Modern-day Sydney is a city of skyscrapers. The Olympic Games will be held here in the year 2000.

Australia Today

Today, the real exploration of Australia is often done by people who never leave their laboratories. Surveys of minerals, metals, new mines and detailed maps are now made with photographs taken from space.

Australia has proved to be an ideal place to explore new forms of energy. Wind and solar power are being used more and more. A race which takes place every year between solar-powered vehicles has become a major international event. The race crosses Australia from Adelaide to Darwin, following the route taken by John McDouall Stuart more than 100 years ago.

Archaeologists, often working with Aboriginal communities, are making exciting discoveries about Australia's prehistoric plant and animal life, and its early human inhabitants. **Anthropologists**, **sociologists** and historians are also making new discoveries about Australian society and culture.

One of the solar-powered vehicles in Australia's solar race.

The monorail in Sydney is a great tourist attraction.

Tourism

A great deal of Australia's modern-day explorers are tourists. More than three million overseas tourists visit Australia each year. These numbers are increasing, and will grow even more when the Olympics are held in Sydney in the year 2000. As well as overseas tourists, more and more Australians are exploring their own country and visiting its national parks and **World Heritage Sites**.

Bushfires remain a danger to Australia's wildlife and people.

Environmental Challenges

Agriculture, sheep grazing and mining have had damaging effects on Australia's environment. Today, soil erosion and salt and water levels in the soil caused by over-farming and chemical fertilizers are serious problems. Many of Australia's unique plants, animals and birds are in danger of dying out and some have already become extinct. One of the greatest challenges facing Australia today is the **conservation** of the environment for future generations.

Melbourne is famous for its trams.

Tourists start to climb Uluru.

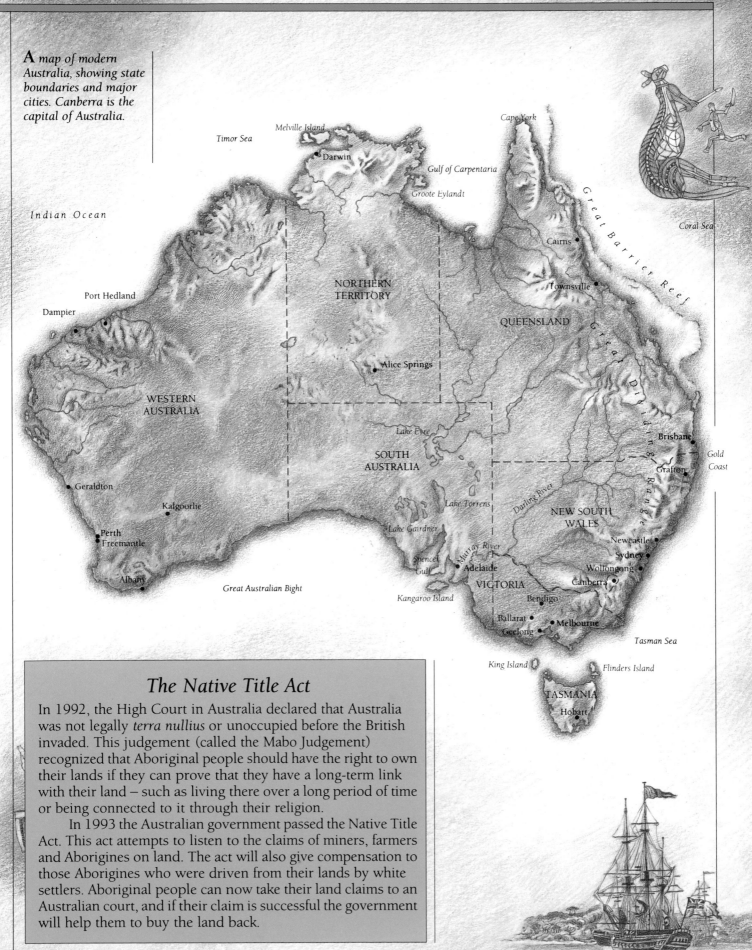

A *map of modern Australia, showing state boundaries and major cities. Canberra is the capital of Australia.*

Timor Sea

Melville Island

Darwin

Gulf of Carpentaria

Groote Eylandt

Cape York

Indian Ocean

Coral Sea

Great Barrier Reef

Cairns

Port Hedland

NORTHERN TERRITORY

QUEENSLAND

Townsville

Dampier

Great Dividing Range

WESTERN AUSTRALIA

Alice Springs

Lake Eyre

Brisbane

Gold Coast

SOUTH AUSTRALIA

Grafton

Geraldton

Lake Torrens

Darling River

NEW SOUTH WALES

Kalgoorlie

Lake Gairdner

Newcastle

Perth
Freemantle

Murray River

Sydney

Spencer Gulf

Adelaide

Wollongong

Canberra

Albany

Great Australian Bight

VICTORIA

Kangaroo Island

Bendigo

Tasman Sea

Ballarat

Melbourne

Geelong

King Island

Flinders Island

TASMANIA

Hobart

The Native Title Act

In 1992, the High Court in Australia declared that Australia was not legally *terra nullius* or unoccupied before the British invaded. This judgement (called the Mabo Judgement) recognized that Aboriginal people should have the right to own their lands if they can prove that they have a long-term link with their land – such as living there over a long period of time or being connected to it through their religion.

In 1993 the Australian government passed the Native Title Act. This act attempts to listen to the claims of miners, farmers and Aborigines on land. The act will also give compensation to those Aborigines who were driven from their lands by white settlers. Aboriginal people can now take their land claims to an Australian court, and if their claim is successful the government will help them to buy the land back.

Australia	Europe	Other
c.50,000 BCE People from Asia, the ancestors of modern Aborigines, migrate to Australia.	**c.6500 BCE** Farming begins in Greece and spreads to other areas of Europe.	**c.5000 BCE** Farming begins in western parts of India.
c.20,000 Evidence that Aborigines are controlling their environment through fire-stick farming.	**c.3000** Use of copper spreads throughout Europe.	**c.2500** The horse is domesticated in Central Asia.
c.12,000 Tasmania separates from the Australian mainland.	**c.1600** Mycenaean civilization begins in Greece.	**c.1200** The Jewish religion emerges. **c.1500** The use of iron begins in Turkey.
c.8000 Papua New Guinea separates from the Australian mainland.	**510** The Roman Republic is founded.	**c.500** The Nok culture in West Africa. **c.600-200** The Paracas culture in Peru.
c.1 CE Population expansion and increase in semi-arid areas throughout Australia.	**43CE** The Roman Empire invades Britain.	**30 CE** Death of Jesus Christ. Spread of Christianity begins.
There are no written records of Aboriginal history during this period. The oral histories of the Aboriginal peoples and archaeological finds tell us that Aboriginal groups created new tools, created social and political organizations and set up trading routes during this time.	**117** The Roman Empire is at its greatest extent.	**300s** The Ghanaian Empire is founded in West Africa.
	c.542 Bubonic plague spreads through Europe.	**622** Mohammed founds the religion of Islam in Arabia.
	959 The Unification of England.	**c.900s** Arabs settle the east coast of Africa. **935** The text of the Quran finished.
	1066 The Normans conquer England.	**c.1000** The Vikings colonize Greenland and travel to America.
	1340s The Bubonic plague continues to spread through Europe.	**c.1345-1530** The Aztec civilization. **1352** Ibn Battuta travels to Africa.
	1492 The first globe is made in Germany by Martin Beheim.	**1498** The Portuguese (led by Vasco da Gama) arrive in India.
	1532 John Calvin starts the Protestant movement in France.	**1530s** The European slave trade begins across the Atlantic Ocean.
1606 Willem Jansz in the *Duyfken* is the first recorded European to land in Australia.	**1618** The Thirty Years War of religion starts.	**1607** The first English settlement is founded in America (Virginia).
c.1700 Trepang fishermen from Macassar regularly visit north Australian coast.	**1667** The French begin to expand under Louis XIV.	**1680** The Rozvi Empire in Zimbabwe.
1770 Captain James Cook claims eastern half of Australia as a British possession.	**1756** The Seven Years War begins. **1789** The French Revolution begins.	**c.1700s** European exploration of Africa. **1775-83** The American Revolution.
1788 First Fleet of convicts arrives at Sydney.	**1807** The slave trade is abolished in Britain.	**1789** George Washington becomes the first President of the United States.
1851 Gold found. Gold rushes begin in New South Wales and Victoria.	**1884-85** The West African conference is held in Berlin (Germany).	**1857** The Indian Mutiny. **1861** The American Civil War begins.
1901 Federation of colonies into one nation. White Australia Policy passed.	**1914-18** World War I.	**1917** The USA enters World War I.
1914-18 World War I.	**1939-45** World War II.	**1941** The USA enters World War II.
1939-45 World War II.	**1961** The Berlin Wall is built in Germany.	**1961** John F. Kennedy becomes President of the USA. **1963** John F. Kennedy is assassinated.
1967 A referendum gives Aborigines full citizenship rights.	**1972** The European Community gains more members.	**1965-73** The USA is involved in the Vietnam War.
1972 A Labour Government introduces self-determination for Aboriginal and Torres Strait Islander peoples.	**1985** Mikhail Gorbachev becomes the leader of the Soviet Union.	**1981** Ronald Reagan becomes the US President.
1993 Native Title Bill passed, recognizing Aboriginal ownership of land prior to 1788.	**1989** Boris Yeltsin becomes leader of Russia. **1991** East and West Germany are united. The Berlin Wall is destroyed.	**1990** Nelson Mandela is released in South Africa. Apartheid begins to break apart. **1993** Bill Clinton becomes the US President.

Glossary

A

Admiralty: the name of the organization that runs the navy of a country.

ancestral spirit beings: in Aboriginal religions these are the beings who created the world and all life in the world.

anthropologist: someone who studies all aspects of human beings.

archaeological: anything that is related to ancient sites and artefacts.

B

baler: the name of a large, open shell that is found in the Pacific Ocean.

botanist: someone who studies plants.

C

circumnavigate: to travel completely around the world.

colonies: lands that are taken over by the government and people of another country.

conservation: the protection of people, animals, plants or places.

convict: someone found guilty of a crime and imprisoned.

D

dialects: a variation of a language spoken by people in one particular place.

dugongs: the name of mammals who live in the sea and are sometimes called sea-cows. Dugongs feed on plants, can grow up to three metres long and can weigh up to 550 kilograms.

Dutch East India Company: a Dutch company formed in the sixteenth century to trade with the East Indies.

E

export: to sell and transport goods, such as food and raw materials, from one country to another.

extinct: something that no longer exists.

F

federal: the name of a type of government. A federal government is a large central government which also allows smaller district or state governments power.

fertile: soil that allows plants to grow in it very easily because it is moist and full of minerals for the plants to feed on.

fibres: very thin threads of material or plant which can be spun with other fibres to make rope or cloth.

G

glacier: a huge river of ice that moves slowly through a landscape carving a path for itself as it advances.

Great Australian Bight: a huge 'dent' in the coast of West and South Australia along the southern half of the Australian continent. This dent is over 1,100 kilometres long and is famous for storms.

guerrilla warfare: a war fought by soldiers who do not belong to an official, national army. Guerrillas use different fighting tactics from official armies, usually involving ambushes and sabotage.

I

Ice Age: a time when the Earth was covered in ice and **glaciers**. There have been several Ice Ages. The first Ice Age took place millions of years ago.

ice cap: an area of permanent ice that is usually found on the top of a mountain or a piece of land.

immigrant: a person who moves to live in a country different from their place of birth.

immunity: the name given to our bodies' ability to resist diseases and illness, such as the common cold and flu.

indigenous: people, plants or animals that live and grow naturally in a certain part of the world.

L

legal: anything to do with law.

M

massacre: the murder of large numbers of people.

marsupial: a type of mammal whose babies grow up in a pouch on the outside of the mother's body.

Ming Dynasty: the Ming family ruled China from 1368 to 1644. This series of rulers is called a dynasty.

mission stations: places set up by **missionaries** to sell food and provisions to people and to teach religion. Mission stations are often in remote places.

missionaries: people who try to convert people from one religion to another.

N

natural science: the name given to any of the sciences concerned with the natural world.

naturalist: someone who studies **botany** and/or zoology (the study of animals).

navigator: someone who can plot a course – this means that they can guide a ship or a plane from one place to another.

P

penal colony: a **colony** of **convicts**.

prehistorians: people who try to investigate the history of human beings and animals before there were written records.

Prussian: someone from Prussia, a state which began in north and central Germany and stretched to France, the Netherlands, the Baltic Sea and Poland. Prussia belonged to Germany.

Ptolemy: a Greek astronomer, geographer and mathematician of the second century CE.

R

rituals: a series of actions (usually associated with religion) of special significance to those who perform them.

Royal Society: a society of scientists founded in Great Britain in 1660 to encourage interest and research in the world of science.

S

semi-traditional lifestyle: one that includes both traditional and modern ways of living.

shearing: cutting off the coat of a sheep with clippers.

sociologist: someone who studies human societies.

spiritual significance: the importance given to a person, place or object by a religion.

survey: to study land in detail.

T

tributaries: a stream or river that joins a larger one.

W

World Heritage Sites: sites recognized by an international organization as having an environment that is unique in the world and which therefore should be protected.

Y

yams: a tropical plant, the root of which is eaten like a vegetable.

Index

Numbers in **bold** indicate an illustration. Words in **bold** are in the glossary on page 37.

First published in Great Britain in 1995 by
Belitha Press Limited
London House, Great Eastern Wharf, Parkgate Road,
London SW11 4NQ

Reprinted 1996
reprinted 1997

Copyright © in this format Belitha Press 1995
Illustrations copyright © Robina Green 1995
Text copyright © Kate Darian-Smith

ISBN 1-85561-362-X

Printed in Hong Kong

British Library Catalogue in Publication Data for this book is available from the British Library

Editor: Jill Laidlaw
Designer: Andrew Oliver
Picture Researcher: Vanessa Kelly
Consultants: Tony Birch and James Bradley
Map overlays: Hardlines

This book ties in with supplementary study units in Key Stage 2 (ages 7-11) and Key Stage 3 (ages 11-14) of the UK National Curriculum.

Photographic credits

Allsport UK Ltd 44 top left; **Ancient Art & Architecture Collection** 6 middle; **Art Gallery of South Australia/ Aboriginal Artists Agency** 17 left; **Australian High Commission, London** 2, 13 bottom, 27 bottom, 37 top and bottom, 39 top left, 42 bottom; **Bridgeman Art Library** 7 left Queensland Art Gallery, Brisbane, 22 bottom National Maritime Museum, 24 top Alecto Historical Editions/British Museum, 25 bottom Royal Geographical Society, 38 top, 39 top right; **Bruce Coleman Ltd** cover foreground, 3, 6 bottom, 9, 11 top left and bottom left, 15 top right, 17 right, 25 top, 44 bottom right; **Mary Evans Picture Library** 20, 29 bottom, 31 right, 33, 36 top; **E.T. Archive** 14 top Queen Victoria Museum, 18 top British Library and bottom, 19 right, 21 top, and bottom National Library of Australia, 22 top, 23 left National Maritime Museum, 26 bottom National Library of Australia, 27 top, 28, 29 top National Library of Australia, 33 bottom, 36 bottom, 38 bottom, 39 bottom, 42 top Australian War Memorial; **Chris Fairclough Colour Library** 37 middle, 41 bottom; **Robert Harding Picture Library** 10, 11 top right, 15 top left, 24 bottom Royal Society, London; **Hulton Deutsch Collection** 12 bottom, 13 top, 14 bottom, 23 right; **Laver Collection, State Library of the Northern Territory** 40 bottom; **Mansell Collection** 19 left, 24 middle, 27 middle, 34 top, 35 left; **Mirror Syndication International** 32 left National Library of Australia; **Mitchell Library, State Library of New South Wales** 30 bottom; **Andrew Oliver** title page, 31 left, 43, 44 top right and bottom left; **John Oxley Library, State Library of Queensland** 35 right; **Royal Geographical Society** 11 top right, 12 top J Miles, 15 bottom J Miles, 30 top, 41 top J Miles, 44 middle left; **Tony Stone Images** cover background, 6 top; **Tasmanian Museum & Art Gallery** 40 top; **University of Melbourne Museum of Art** back cover; **Zefa Picture Library** 7 right.